- To my children -

Elisha, Davida, Yadin,
Nadav, and Safira

To Rachel, who is my Desire and who I keep rediscovering.
To Krishnapriya, for being with me every step of the way.

Originally published in the United States by Jean-Pierre Weill Studios
The Library of Congress has cataloged the original Jean-Pierre Weill Studios edition as follows:

LCCN: 2012914015

Flatiron Books ISBN 978-1-250-09270-0 (hardcover)
Flatiron Books ISBN 978-1-250-09272-4 (e-book)

Our books may be purchased in bulk for promotional, educational, or business use.
Please contact your local bookseller or the Macmillan Corporate and Premium Sales Department
at (800) 221-7945, extension 5442, or by e-mail at MacmillanSpecialMarkets@macmillan.com.

Cover and book design: Emmanuel Yadin Klein

First Flatiron Books Edition: November 2016

10 9 8 7 6 5 4 3 2

thewellofbeing.co

The Well of Being

a children's book for adults

Written and illustrated by
Jean-Pierre Weill

Edited by Margaret Osburn
Designed by Emmanuel Yadin Klein

FLATIRON
BOOKS
NEW YORK

In memory of Tanielle Gavre'a Margalit

(1986-2005)

preFace

(*The preface is a teaching of Ramchal, the 18th Century Italian philosopher and mystic.*)

In the beginning there was nothing.

Only Oneness.

all**O**ne

There arose within Oneness a desire, so to speak, to bestow a gift. So It chose to give Itself, since It alone was real.

all ne

A space in the nothing was surrendered, and

BANG! The universe was created. An event not very easy to illustrate.

Within the new universe each creation was
given the gift of oneness.

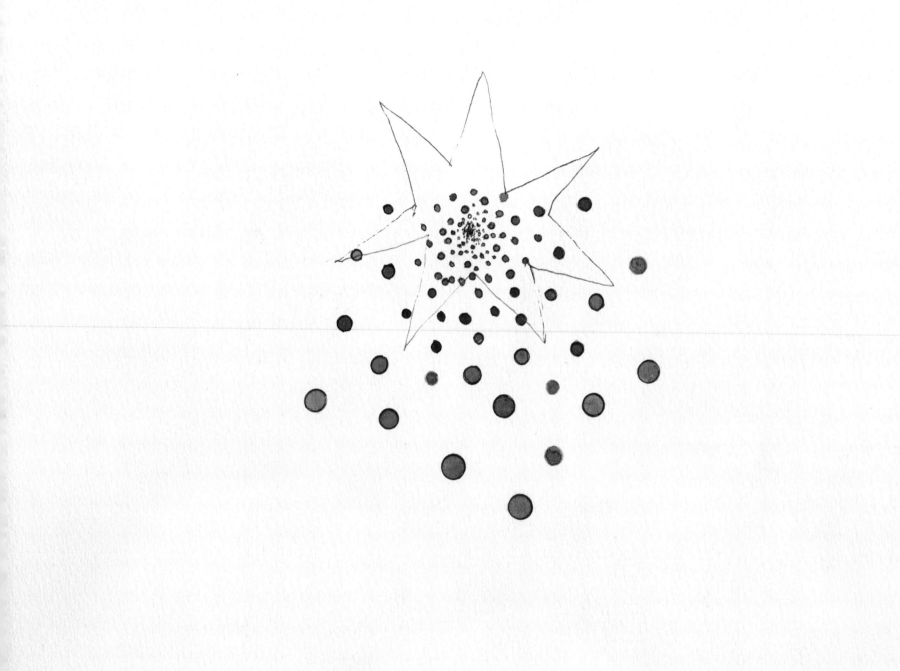

They joined into more complex wholes,

until the most novel and distinctive beings emerged.
Yet none had awakened to the gift they had received.

THE STORY

I see that you're reading.

As the train is late

let me take you on an excursion

to the place we long for.

I ask of you one thing: bring
attention to your thoughts, those that take
you from this book, quiet them...

and value this listening
as if it were a mysterious gift

yours for the taking.

Let us string a bead of thought,
an article of faith.

Within us, beneath the noise,

at the source and core of everything

is a mysterious One, which gives
everything its separate existence.

It is always available. We may call our encounter with One, *well-being*.

Many illustrious voices say this is not so.
An encounter with our source, they say, is illusory.

At the crux of things, they reason,
everything is random.

Life is reduced to matter,

and freedom is reduced to necessity.

In their view there is no well-being nor gift to be had.

Heroic though it may be, theirs is not our path.

Our path is one

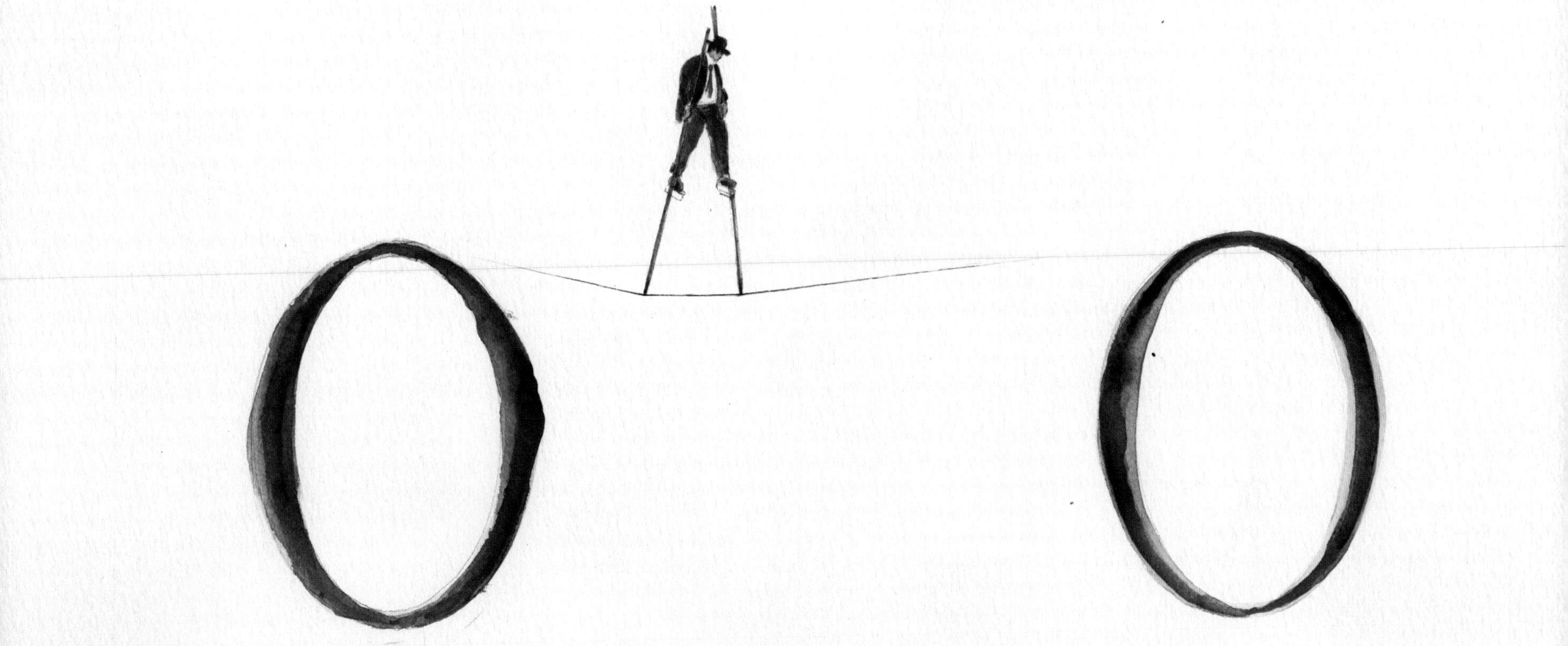

in which our existence is not an accident

but a mystery. Mystery of the
encounter with One.

We can entrust ourselves to this mystery,
for we are part of it. Indeed we are it.

I don't say there isn't much work to do, for there is.

And some tracks lead to excruciating darkness,

where a person can tumble from the sky on a
clear September morning.

Yet is the world not whole? Is it not beautiful?

For now, let's consider well-being a choice, something you can try on and wear. When we put on the hat and coat of well-being

we incline towards joy without special occasion.

We value others and are happy to show it.

We appreciate the fleeting and marginal
things scattered everywhere.

We feel our feelings and release them.

And when there's drama about,

we remain at home in the world.

In well-being, we flow. We know that

to be I is a gift.

When we lose touch with well-being,

joy seems to depend on circumstance, on what happens outside of us.

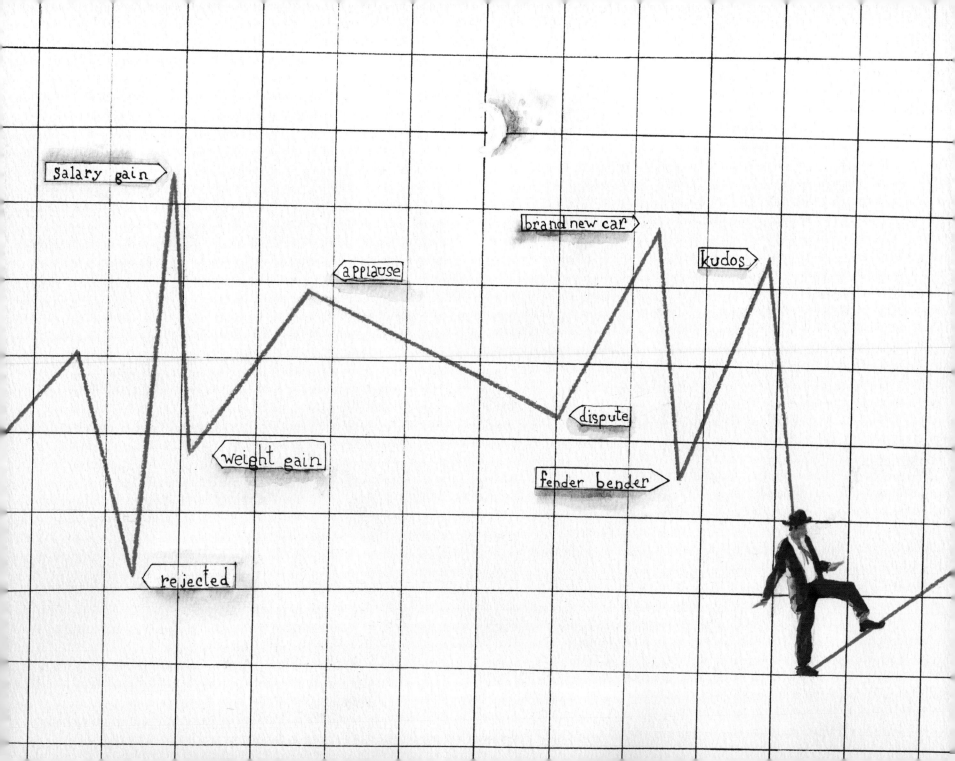

No longer at home in the world, we experience it as a battleground and people as adversaries.

We feel cut off,

with few choices,

and turn the battle against ourselves.

Trapped by concepts,

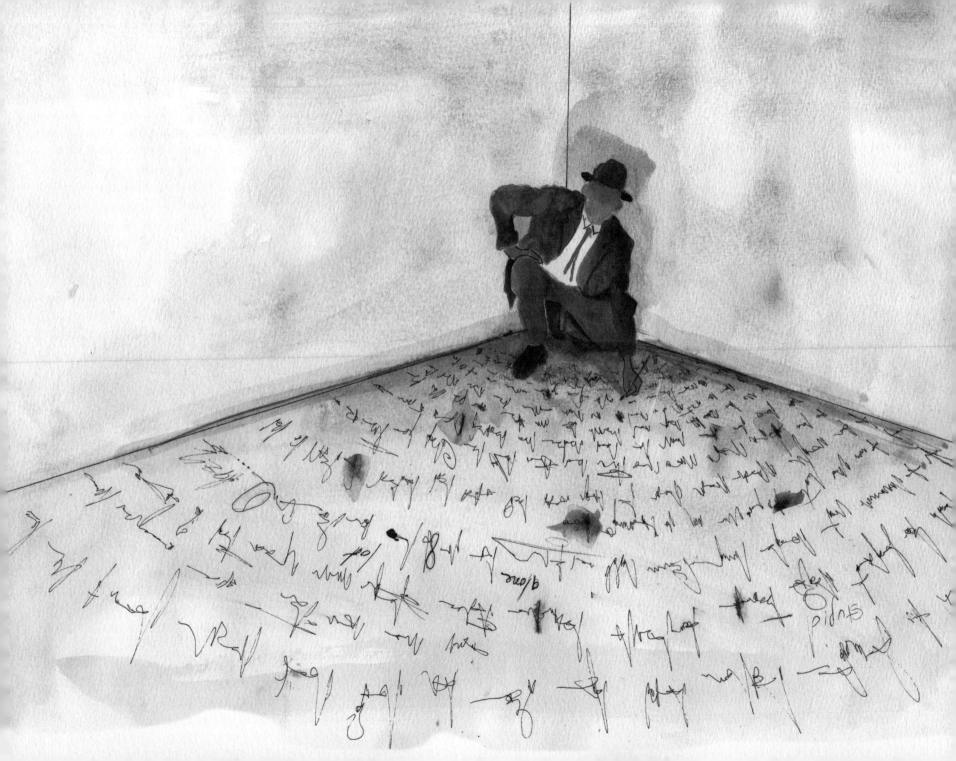

we weave epics about past glories and failures,
or failures and glories to come.

We wonder, "Where has it gone?

Indeed did I ever have well-being?"

Let us thread another bead and find out where it went.

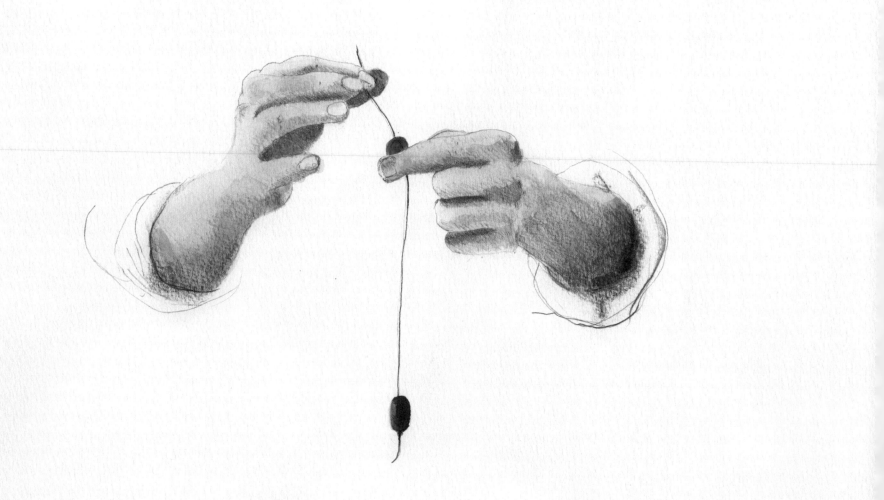

Once upon a time

when we were infants in the garden,
with no thought to be anything other than ourselves,

we lived in the sanctuary of One, without even knowing it. There was neither good or bad nor right or wrong. The world was whole.

And whatever we made was a masterpiece.

One day the child that was us passed by an empty wall. A picture would be splendid here.

Five trees, four birds, three stars, two deer,
one moon...

Then, footsteps! "*A wonderful surprise is coming,*" he thought.

Oh!
What a discovery!

But it was he who would make the discovery
- *the* discovery - that he could do something wrong.

That he, or the world, could *be* wrong.

And that he was alone. From then on

he practiced ways to rearrange himself, to make himself acceptable so that he could return home.

And so it continues. For the train is running late.

And people are waiting.
And things may go wrong.

Circumstances are wrong. They seem to ferry our well-being up and down, round and round.

If our circumstances are wrong
how can we possibly ascend to well-being?

Let us thread our final bead

and stand the matter on its head.

Well-being is generated not from the outside
but from the inside.

We organize our circumstances into stories,

stories we pick up along the way

and carry within us.

Stories that declare, *I'm lacking.*

Why me? stories.

I'm alone, stories.

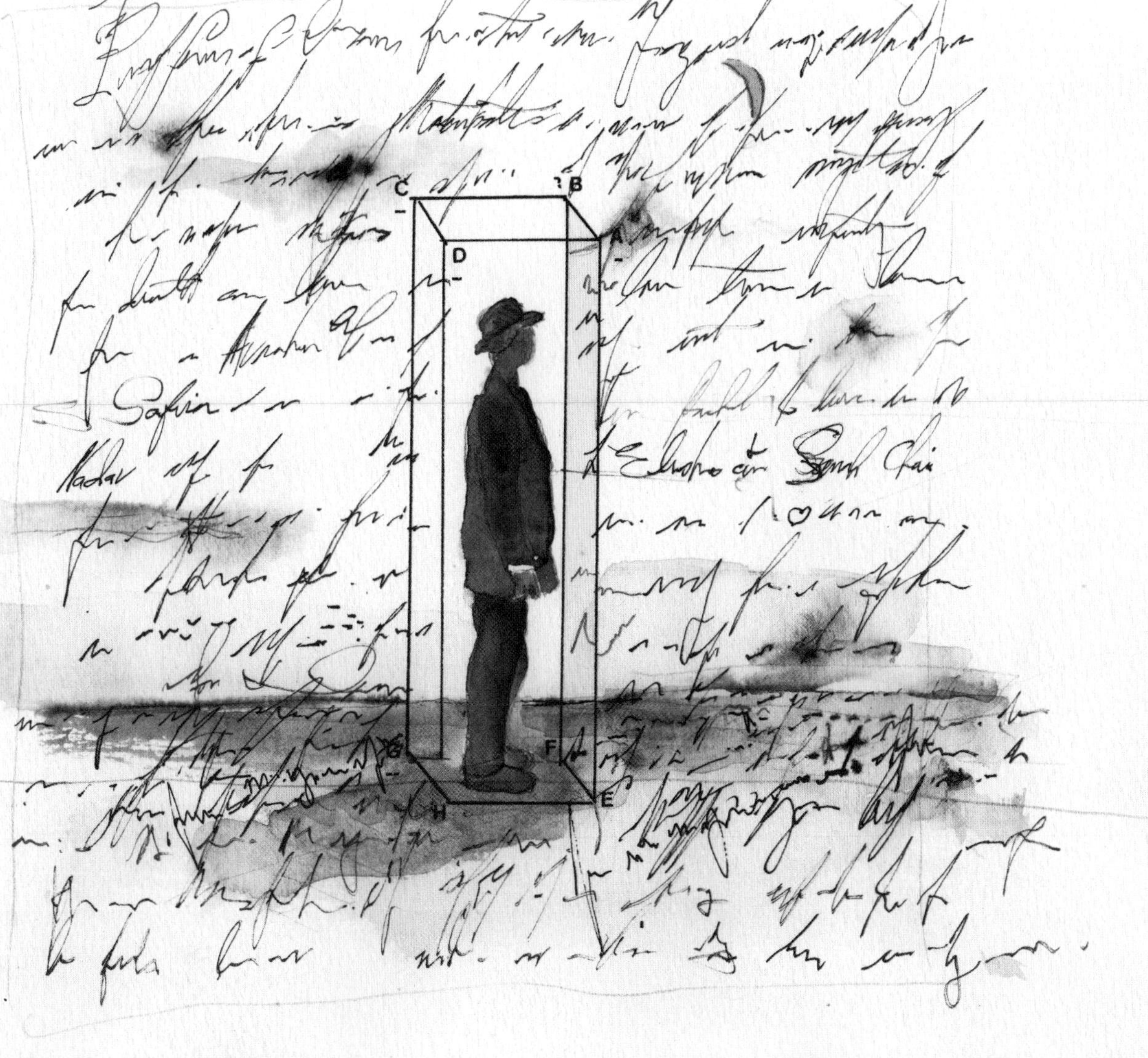
C
B
D
A
G
F
H
E

What will I amount to? stories.

Stories about who we should be.

Or think we are.

They are interior maps
whose familiar roads we travel.

If you love me; Sorry I'm not Picasso or Proust

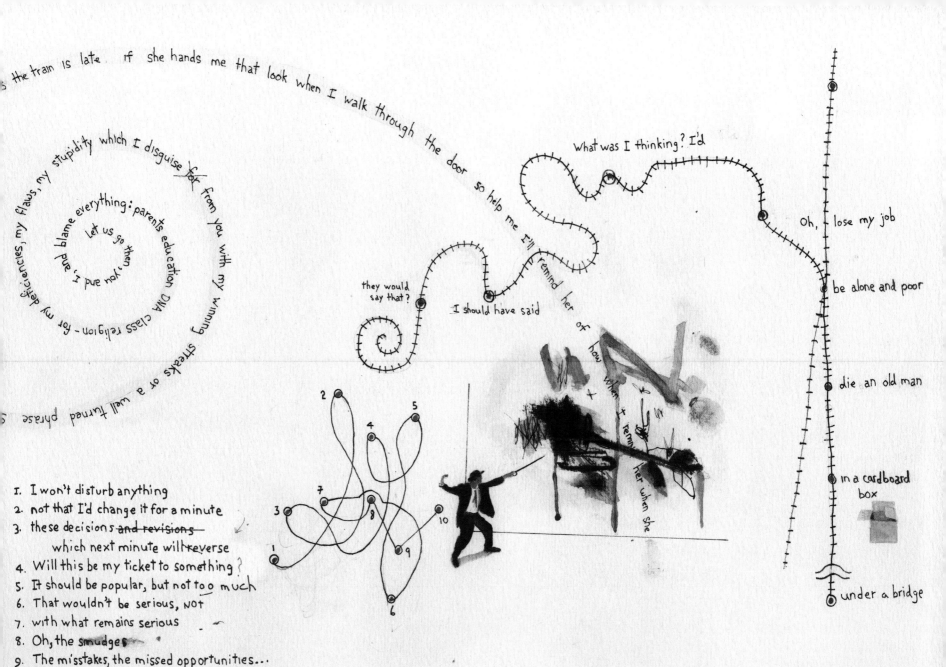

Over and over.

Yet when we apprehend these maps,
these stories, these patterns,

when we become aware of our own thinking,

we awaken

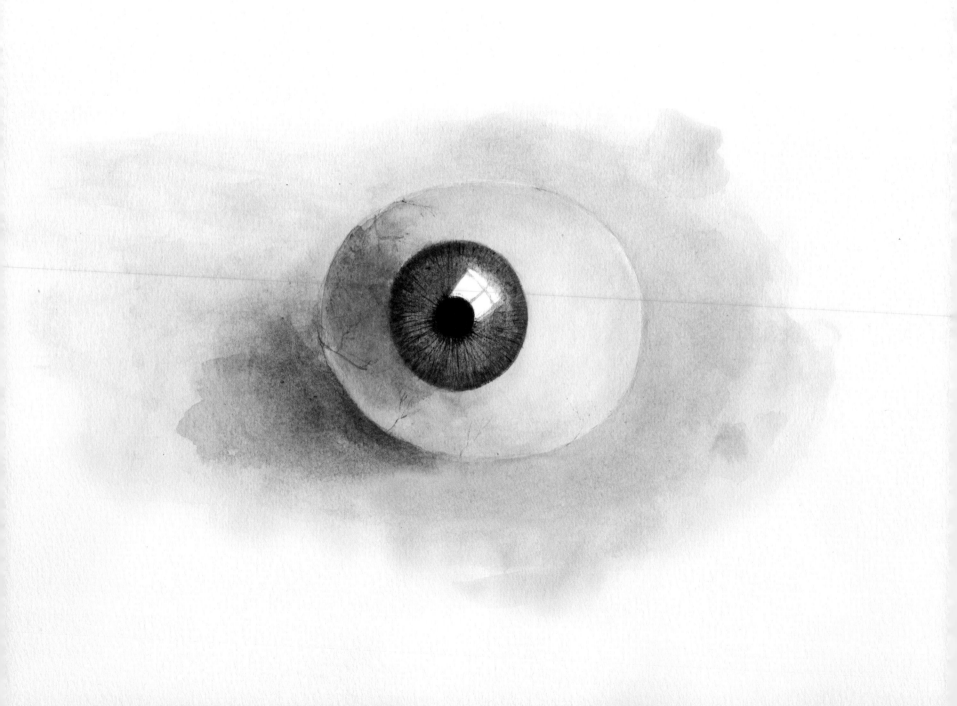

and arise, as it were,

to a new perspective, to new possibilities.
We see that our misery

had only been us looking through the stories with
which we had defined the world;

and our difficult feelings simply our body's
responses to those narratives.

A W H H H

From here, Oh, you can hold yourself, you can laugh.

Free to explore all manners of things.

When you're here, an i in the O-

cean,

you're no longer waiting
for something to happen or to change.

When you're here you have what you seek.

Your heart opens

to the gift you receive, that you are.

You are drinking at the well

of being.

Endnotes

Page ix	*Ramchal*	Moshe Chaim Luzzatto (1707 - 1746), a Jewish luminary whose chief teachings concern man's fundamental relationship to Creation.
Page xxiii	*Cell*	Within the Western spiritual tradition the number seven represents both the natural world order and the notion of wholeness, completeness. A week has six days and a Sabbath. In space, every existent abides in six directions and has a center.
Page 3	*Charan*	The place where the Patriarch Abraham settled temporarily on his journey to the land of Canaan.
	Poster	The poster on the train station wall shows a conceptual map of the *Tree of Life*, known in kabbalah as *Sephirot*. The *Sephirot* represent the building blocks of Creation.
Page 23	חסד	Pronounced *khesed*, is a Hebrew word closely associated with loving-kindness. Jewish tradition assigns it as the primary virtue and considers it the foundational quality with which the world is created.
	ǝʌˌloʌǝ	I believe evolution to be based in love.
Page 29	*D. W. Guy*	Dead White Guy
	תהו	Pronounced *tohu*, is a Hebrew word associated with formless chaos. It imagines the world before creation in the book of Genesis (1:2).
Page 33	*Guernica*	Picasso's iconic *Guernica* depicts life wrenched by violence and chaos.
	Campbell's Soup	Andy Warhol's deadpan *Campbell's Soup Can* seems an appropriate bookend to Guernica.
Page 37	*Man Pointing*	Jean-Paul Sartre called Giacometti's gaunt figures "halfway between nothingness and being". This sculpture's index figure is modified to an upturned middle finger, echoing the cynicism that often accompanies modernist existentialism.

Page 41	*1954*	Author's date of birth.
Page 49	*Auschwitz*	Auschwitz is a concentration-camp in Nazi-occupied Poland which operated from 1940 - 1945. More than one million people were transported by train and slaughtered there.
Page 51	*9/11*	The drawing is based on a photograph taken by Richard Drew of an unknown man who jumped to his death from the World Trade Center on September 11, 2001.
Page 71	*"I"*	The man stands in the form of the upper-case letter "I", which here represents the Higher Self.
Page 103	*Neoplasticism*	The painting on the wall by Piet Mondrian is a depiction of structure and order.
Page 109	*Angel*	The painting on the bedroom wall is from Gustave Doré's illustration of Adam being driven out of the Garden of Eden. Adam's expulsion represents the individual's evolution from undifferentiated union with the world to separation from the world as an individuated self.
	American Gothic	The framed picture on the stand is based on Grant Wood's depiction of traditional puritan American values.
Page 113	*דין*	Pronounced *din*, is a Hebrew word closely associated with the concept of judgment. It provides every existent with definition and identity.
Page 161	*תפארת*	Pronounced *tiferet*, is a Hebrew word associated with the concept of beauty or harmony. It relates the part to the whole, such as a note relates to the melody, or a moment in a life relates to its larger context or story. *Tiferet* brings perspective.
Page 171	*"i"*	The drop of water forms the lower-case "i", which here represents the lower self.

Attributions and Thanks to

Page xiii   **ee cummings**, who raised a single letter to the upper case: alOne

Page 23   **Horacio Cardozo**, who inspired the image of a hoop's heart-shaped shadow.

Pages 35, 59, 89 **Saul Steinberg**, who inspires so much in this book, surveyed the space between imagery and text.

Page 43   **Paul Klee's** humor, musicality, and childlike perspective exert influence on many of my illustrations.

Page 53   **Kenneth Noland**, colorist, made beautiful circles.

Page 75   **Volker Kühn**, a German craft artist, points out to me how to create visual slogans about the quandaries of modern life.

Page 97   **Charles Wilson Peale's** painting, *The Artist in His Museum*, gave me the idea for pulling back the curtain of our child's story.

Page 113   **Advard Munch's** *The Scream*, may indeed be the *Mona Lisa* of modern times.

Page 123   **Robert and Shana ParkeHarrison** inspired me with their fabulous *Flying Lesson* in *The Architect's Brother*.

Page 135, 149   **T.S. Eliot's** *The Love Song of J. Alfred Prufrock* surfaces throughout the book in little ways. Mr Prufrock exemplifies modern man's gloomy state of mind.

                 Shel Silverstein's *The Giving Tree* is a classic children's book rendered with simple line drawings and text. It evokes in the reader complex and competing emotions.